Published By Robert Corbin

@ Clarence Nixon

The Sirtfood Diet: Natural Health Benefits and Burn Fat, Lose Weight Fast and Activate Your Skinny Gene

All Right RESERVED

ISBN 978-87-94477-32-1

TABLE OF CONTENTS

pasta Salad With Heirloom Tomatoes And Pan-Roasted Zucchini 1

Artichoke, Chicken, And Capers 5

Chicken Merlot With Mushrooms 7

Country Chicken Breasts 9

Turkey With Sirtfood Vegetables 12

Cauliflower Couscous And Turkey Steak 14

Sirtfood Lamb 16

Raspberry & Kale Salad 18

Cucumber & Onion Salad 20

Turmeric Baked Salmon 21

Sirtfood Turkey Wrap 24

Salmon Salad 26

Fragrant Hotpot 28

Lamb, Butternut Squash And Date Tagine 31

Chocolate Granola 35

Buckwheat With Coconut And Nuts 37

Simple Celery Juice 39

Kale, Apple, And Celery Juice 40

Citrus Fruit Salad 41

Mixed Berries Salad 43

Shakshuka Oriental Vegetable Stew With Eggs 44

Vegetable And Lentil Stew With Peas 47

Strawberry Buckwheat Tabouleh 50

Sirtfood Bites 51

Chocolate Cupcakes With Matcha Icing 54

Sesame Chicken Salad 58

Lamb, Butternut Squash And Date Taginesirtfood Recipes 60

Prawn Arrabbiata-Sirtfood Recipes 64

Baked Salmon Salad With Creamy Mint Dressing 67

Choc Chip Granola 70

Bumper Oat Cookies 72

Roast Tomatoes With Asparagus & Black Olives 75

Stuffed Peppers With Buckwheat 77

Blueberry Salad With Crispy Tempeh Strips.................. 80

Grilled Leeks With Pomegranate Vinaigrette................. 82

Tattooed Potatoes With Rosemary............................... 86

Salad Smoothie.. 88

Avocado Kale Smoothie 89

Prawn Stir Fry 90

Chicken Zucchini Stir Fry 92

Sirtfood Lentil Soup.. 95

Grilled Steak With Roasted Vegetables.......................... 98

Miso-Marinated Baked Cod With Stir-Fried Greens & Sesame 101

Prawn Arrabbiata 104

Mixed Berry Yogurt 107

Salsa Bean Dip 108

Creamy Sunshine Smoothie 109

Blueberries And Coconut Smoothie 110

Butternut Pumpkin With Buckwheat 112

Chicken And Kale With Spicy Salsa 115

Cottage Cheese With Fruit 118

Tea-Cake 120

Choc Chip Granola 123

Strawberries Cream 126

Apples And Plum Cake 127

Garlic Chilli Prawns With Sesame Noodles 129

Superhealthy Salmon Salad 132

Malabar Prawns 134

Zucchini Noodles With Vegetables And Sour Cream ... 136

PASTA SALAD WITH HEIRLOOM TOMATOES AND PAN-ROASTED ZUCCHINI

Ingredients:

For the pan-roasted zucchinis

- 2 tablespoons extra virgin olive oil

- 3 baby zucchinis about 6" long ends trimmed and cut in 1/2" dices

- 1/4 teaspoon sea salt

For the pasta

- 6 tablespoons extra virgin olive oil

- 2 lbs 907gr red, purple or black heirloom tomatoes seeded and cut in 1/2" dices

- 1 bunch fresh chives cut in 1/4" slices use kitchen scissors

- 24 large basil leaves torn in 1" pieces

- 1 tablespoon sea salt for the pasta water

- 1 lb 454gr mezzi rigatoni, penne rigate, ziti or ditali pasta

- 7 oz 198gr goat milk feta cheese crumbled

- 2 ears fresh sweet corn husks removed

- 2 garlic cloves skinned and crushed use microplane grater

- 1 1/4 teaspoons sea salt or to taste

- Freshly ground black pepper to taste

- 2 teaspoons aged balsamic vinegar

- Small basil leaves as garnish

Directions:

1. Heat a wide skillet over medium-high heat. Add the extra virgin olive oil and zucchinis. Sauté for 7 to 8 minutes, until golden-brown,

tossing only occasionally. Sprinkle with the salt. Toss again and transfer to a bowl to cool. Set aside.
2. Fill a large pot with water and bring to a boil. Add the corn and boil for 3 minutes. Remove from pot and transfer to a bowl filled with cold water. As soon as the corn has cooled, transfer to a clean kitchen towel and pat dry. Using a sharp knife, shave the kernels from the corn. Set aside.
3. In a large bowl, place the garlic, salt, pepper, vinegar and oil. Whisk until well blended. Add the corn, tomatoes, chives and basil. Toss until well mixed and set aside.
4. Bring 6 quarts of water to a boil. When the water is boiling, add 1 tablespoon of salt and the pasta.
5. Cook pasta according to package instructions, until very al dente about 1 minute less than what package calls for.

6. Drain and rinse with cold water until cooled. Shake off the excess water. Add to the tomato mixture. Mix well and let stand at room temperature for 15 to 30 minutes before serving.
7. When ready to serve Add the pan-roasted zucchini to the pasta and stir well. Spoon pasta into individual bowls or a large serving platter.
8. Crumble the feta on top and garnish with small basil leaves. Drizzle with a little more extra virgin olive oil if desired. Finish with freshly ground black pepper and serve.

Artichoke, Chicken, and Capers

Ingredients:

- 1 medium yellow onion, diced
- ½ cup Kalamata olives, sliced
- ¼ cup capers, drained
- 3 tablespoons chia seeds
- 3 teaspoons curry powder
- 1 teaspoon turmeric
- 3/4 teaspoon dried lovage
- 6 b2less, skinless chicken breasts
- 2 cups mushrooms, sliced
- 1 14 ½ ounces can diced tomatoes
- 1 8 or 9 ounces package frozen artichokes

- 1 cup chicken broth
- ¼ cup dry white wine
- Salt and pepper to taste
- 3 cups hot cooked buckwheat

Directions:
1. Rinse chicken & put aside.
2. In a large bowl, combine mushrooms, tomatoes with juice, frozen artichoke hearts, chicken stock, wine, onion, olives, and capers.
3. Stir in chia seeds, flavorer, turmeric, lovage, salt, and pepper.
4. Pour 1 the mixture into your crockpot, add the chicken, and pour the rest of the sauce over the top.
5. Cover and cook on Low for 7 to eight hours or on High for 3 1/2 to 4 hours.
6. Serve with hot cooked buckwheat.
7. Rinse chicken & set aside.

Chicken Merlot with Mushrooms

Ingredients:

- ¼ cup Merlot
- 3 tablespoons chia seeds
- 2 tablespoons basil, chopped finely
- 2 teaspoons sugar
- Salt and pepper to taste
- 1 10 ounces package buckwheat ramen noodles, cooked
- 2 tablespoons Parmesan, shaved
- 6 b2less, skinless chicken breasts, cubed
- 3 cups mushrooms, sliced
- 1 large red onion, chopped

- 2 cloves garlic, minced
- ¾ cup chicken broth
- 1 6 ounces can tomato paste

Directions:

1. Rinse chicken; put aside.
2. Add mushrooms, onion, and garlic to the crockpot and blend.
3. Place chicken cubes on top of the vegetables and don't mix.
4. In a large bowl, combine broth, ingredient, wine, chia seeds, basil, sugar, salt, and pepper. Pour over the chicken.
5. Cover and cook on low for 7 to eight hours or on high for 3 ½ to 4 hours.
6. To serve, spoon chicken, mushroom mixture, and sauce over hot cooked buckwheat ramen noodles. Top with shaved Parmesan.

Country Chicken Breasts

Ingredients:

- 1 teaspoon ground ginger

- ¼ Teaspoon chili pepper flakes

- 1 can 14 ½ ounce diced tomatoes

- 6 skinless, b2less chicken breasts, halved

- ½ Cup chicken broth

- 1 cup long-grain white rice

- 1 pound large raw shrimp, shelled and deveined

- Salt and pepper to taste

- 2 medium green apples, diced

- 1 small red onion, finely diced

- 1 small green bell pepper, chopped
- 3 cloves garlic, minced
- 2 tablespoons dried currants
- 1 tablespoon curry powder
- 1 teaspoon turmeric
- Chopped parsley
- 1/3 cup slivered almonds

Directions:
1. Rinse chicken, pat dry, and put aside.
2. In a large crockpot, combine apples, onion, bell pepper, garlic, currants, flavorer, turmeric, ginger, and chili pepper flakes. Stir in tomatoes.
3. Arrange chicken, overlapping pieces slightly, on top of tomato mixture.
4. Pour in broth and don't mix or stir.

5. Cover and cook for six 7 hours on low.
6. Preheat oven to 200 degrees F.
7. Carefully transfer chicken to an oven-safe plate, cover lightly, and keep warm In the oven.
8. Stir rice into the remaining liquid. Increase cooker heat setting to high; cover and cook, stirring once or twice until rice is nearly tender to bite, 30 to 35 minutes. Stir in shrimp, cover, and cook until shrimp are opaque in center, about ten more minutes.
9. Meanwhile, toast almonds In a small pan over medium heat until golden brown, 5 - 8 minutes, stirring occasionally. Set aside.
10. To serve, season rice mixture to taste with salt and pepper. Mound In a warm dish and arrange chicken on top. Sprinkle with parsley and almonds.

TURKEY WITH SIRTFOOD VEGETABLES

Ingredients:

- 1 tsp of finely chopped ginger

- Extra virgin olive oil, 2 tbsp

- Ground turmeric, 1 tbsp

- ½ cup of dried tomatoes

- Parsley, 10 g

- Sage, dried, 1 tsp

- ½ juiced lime or lemon

- Lean turkey meat, 150 g

- 1 finely chopped garlic clove

- 1 finely chopped red onion

- 1 finely chopped bird's eye chili/replace with chopped red bell paprika or ½ squeezed citrus fruit if you don't like spicy foods

- Capers, 1 tbsp

Directions:

1. Chop the cauliflower. Fry with cleaved ginger, bean stew, red onion, and garlic in 1 tbsp olive oil until they're delicate.
2. Add cauliflower and turmeric, and cook for several minutes until the cauliflower turns out to be delicate. When the dish is d2, add dried tomatoes and parsley.
3. Coat your turkey in a meager layer of olive oil and sage. Fry for around five minutes, and afterward include the tricks and lime juice. Add a large portion of some water and bring to a boil

CAULIFLOWER COUSCOUS AND TURKEY STEAK

Ingredients:

- 150 g turkey steak 1 tsp dried sage Juice of ½ lemon 1 tbsp tricks

- 40 g red onion, finely cut

- 1 bird's eye chili, finely sliced 1 tsp cleaved new ginger 2 tbsp additional virgin olive oil

- 150 g cauliflower, generally cut 1 garlic clove, finely sliced

- 2 tsp ground turmeric

- 30 g sun-dried tomatoes, finely sliced 10g parsley

Directions:

1. Deteriorate the cauliflower using a food processor. Blend in 1-2 pulses until the

cauliflower has a breadcrumb-like consistency.
2. In a skillet, fry garlic, stew, ginger, and red onion in 1 tsp olive oil for In a skillet, fry garlic, stew, ginger, and red onion in 1 tsp olive oil for 3 minutes.
3. Throw in the turmeric and cauliflower by then cook for another 1-2 minutes.
4. Eliminate from warmth and incorporate the tomatoes and for the most part a huge piece of the parsley.
5. Embellishment the turkey steak with savvy and dress with oil. In a dish, over medium warmth, fry the turkey steak for 5 minutes, turning unexpectedly.
6. At the point when the steak is cooked incorporate lemon juice, stunts, and a scramble of water. Blend and present with the couscous.

SIRTFOOD LAMB

Ingredients:

- Cumin seeds, 2 tsp

- 1 cinnamon stick

- Lamb, 800 g

- Garlic cloves, crushed, 3 pieces A pinch of salt

- Chopped Medjool dates, 1 cup Chickpeas, 400 g

- Coriander, 2 tbsp

- Extra virgin olive oil, 2 tbsp

- Grated ginger, 2 inch

- 1 sliced red onion.

- 1 tsp of bird's eye

- Buckwheat

Directions:
1. Start by preheating your stove to 140 ºC. Sauté cut onion with 2 tbsp of additional virgin olive oil for five minutes while keeping the top on. The onions should turn delicate yet not brown.
2. Add turmeric, cumin, ginger, garlic, and bean stew and pan fried food for another minute.
3. Add the pieces of sheep, season with salt and let, and let bubble. Add a glass of water.
4. After the blend has bubbled, cook in the broiler for 2 hour and 15 minutes. Add the chickpeas 30 minutes before the dish is finished.
5. Add cleaved coriander and present with buckwheat after the feast is d2.

Raspberry & Kale Salad

Ingredients:

For the salad:

- ½ cup fresh raspberries

- ¼ cup walnuts, chopped

- 3 cups fresh baby kale

For the dressing:

- ½ teaspoon pure maple syrup

- Salt and ground black pepper, as required

- 1 tablespoon extra-virgin olive oil

- 1 tablespoon apple cider vinegar

Directions:

1. For the salad: in a salad bowl, place all the Ingredients:and mix.

2. For the dressing: place all the Ingredients:in another bowl and beat until well combined.
3. Place dressing on top of the salad and toss to coat thoroughly.
4. Serve immediately.

Cucumber & Onion Salad

Ingredients:

- 2 tablespoons olive oil
- 1 tablespoon fresh apple cider vinegar
- Sea salt, to taste
- ¼ cup fresh parsley, chopped
- 3 large cucumbers, sliced thinly
- ½ cup red onion, sliced

Directions:
1. In a salad bowl, place all the Ingredients:and toss to coat thoroughly.
2. Serve immediately.

Turmeric Baked Salmon

Ingredients:

- 1 clove of garlic, minced
- 1 bird's eye chili, minced remove seeds if you do not like spicy foods
- 1 ½ cups chopped celery
- 1 teaspoon curry powder more to taste if you prefer it spicy
- ½ cup of chicken stock
- 1 tablespoon chopped parsley
- 14 ounces piece of salmon, skinned
- 1 teaspoon olive oil
- 1 teaspoon turmeric powder
- ¼ lemon, juiced

- ½ cup diced red onion
- 1/3 cup canned green lentils
- 1 ½ small whole tomatoes, diced

Directions:

1. Preheat your oven to 400 degrees Fahrenheit.
2. Add olive oil to a frying pan on medium-low heat and wait until oil is shimmering. Then, add in onion, garlic, celery, ginger, and chili.
3. Gently sauté for 2 or 3 minutes until it is softened. Then, add the curry powder and cook for another minute.
4. Add in the tomato, then the stock and finally, add in the lentils. Then, cook on low heat at a low simmer for 10 minutes. Check the texture of the celery to determine preference.
5. Mix turmeric, lemon juice, and oil together in a small bowl, then rub it on the salmon. Add it to a baking tray and cook for 10 minutes, or until flaking

6. Add parsley to the celery and serve with the salmon.

Sirtfood Turkey Wrap

Ingredients:

- 1/4 cup mixed greens
- 1/4 cup chopped cucumber
- 1/4 cup hummus
- 4 oz sliced turkey breast
- 1 whole-grain tortilla

Drections:

1. Lay the whole-grain tortilla flat on a plate or cutting board.
2. Spread the hummus evenly over the tortilla.
3. Add the mixed greens and chopped cucumber on top of the hummus.
4. Place the sliced turkey breast on top of the vegetables.

5. Roll the tortilla tightly around the fillings, tucking in the sides as you go.
6. Cut the wrap in 1 diagonally, if desired.
7. Serve and enjoy!

Salmon Salad

Ingredients:

- 4 oz grilled salmon
- 1/4 cup sliced almonds
- 1 tbsp balsamic vinegar
- 2 cups mixed greens
- 1/2 cup cherry tomatoes

Drections:

1. Rinse the mixed greens and pat them dry.
2. Cut the cherry tomatoes in 1.
3. In a large bowl, combine the mixed greens and cherry tomatoes.
4. Break the grilled salmon into small pieces and add to the bowl.
5. Sprinkle sliced almonds on top of the salad.
6. Drizzle the balsamic vinegar over the salad.

7. Toss the salad gently until all Ingredients: are mixed well.
8. Serve and enjoy!

Fragrant Hotpot

Ingredients:

- 1 carrot (peeled & cut into matchsticks)
- 50grams broccoli (cut into small florets)
- A small handful of parsley (10grams, stalks finely chopped)
- 50grams beansprouts
- 20grams sushi ginger (chopped)
- 100grams raw tiger prawns
- 1/4 teaspoon of ground anise or 2 star anise (crushed)
- 2 teaspoon of tomato purée
- A small handful of coriander (10grams, stalks finely chopped

- 50grams cooked water chestnuts (drained)
- 1 of lime juice
- 100grams firm tofu, (chopped)
- 2 tablespoon of good-quality miso paste
- 500ml chicken stock (either fresh or made with 2 cube)
- 50grams rice noodles (cooked according to Directions: on pack)

Directions:

1. Place the star anise, tomato purée, coriander stalks, parsley stalks, chicken stock and lime juice in a clean big pan and then bring to a simmer for about ten mins.
2. Add the broccoli, carrot, tofu, noodles, water chestnuts and prawns and gently simmer until the prawns are well cooked.
3. Take away from the heat and then stir in the miso paste and sushi ginger.
4. You should serve sprinkled with the coriander leaves and parsley.

Lamb, Butternut Squash And Date Tagine

Ingredients:

- 2 cinnamon stick
- 3 teaspoons of ground turmeric
- 800grams lamb neck fillet (cut into chunks about 2-cm)
- Buckwheat, couscous, flatbreads or rice (Serving purpose)
- 100grams medjool dates (pitted & chopped)
- 400grams tin chickpeas (drained)
- 1 teaspoon of salt
- 2 red onion (sliced)
- 3 tablespoons of olive oil
- 4 garlic cloves (either grated or crushed)

- 400grams tin chopped tomatoes, plus 1 a can of water

- 2 teaspoon of chilli flakes (or as desired)

- 3 tablespoons of fresh coriander (plus extra for garnish)

- 2-cm ginger (grated)

- 500grams butternut squash (chopped into 1-cm cubes)

- 3 teaspoons of cumin seeds

Directions:
1. Heat up the oven to 140 degrees C.
2. In a clean large ovenproof saucepan or cast iron casserole dish drizzle about two tablespoons of olive oil.
3. Afterwards, add the sliced onion, with the lid on cook on a gentle heat for approximately

five minutes, until the onions becomes soften but isn't brown.
4. Add the ginger and grated garlic, cumin, chilli, turmeric and cinnamon. Stir and then cook for additional 2 minute with the lid off.
5. If it gets too dry you can add a splash of water.
6. Add in the lamb chunks. Stir slowly to coat the meat in the spices and onions, afterwards, add the chopped dates, tomatoes and salt, and also about 1 a can of water.
7. Bring the tagine to the boil, having d2 that, put the lid on and place in the heated oven for 1 hr 15 mins.
8. When it is about 30 minutes to the end of the cooking time, add in the drained chickpeas and chopped butternut squash. Stir all, put the lid back on and then return to the oven for the last time, About 30 mins.

9. When the tagine is set, take out of the oven and then stir through the chopped coriander. You should serve with couscous, buckwheat, basmati rice or flatbreads.

Chocolate Granola

Ingredients:

- 70% cocoa chocolate chips 1 cup
- Brown sugar 2 tablespoon
- Butter 2 and a 1 tablespoon
- Walnuts ¼ cup (chopped)
- Organic oats 2 and a 1 cup
- Extra-virgin olive oil 4 tablespoons
- Maple syrup 2 tablespoons

Directions:

1. Preheat your oven to 160 degrees F and line your baking tray with parchment paper.
2. Mix the chopped walnuts and oats in a bowl and set aside.

3. Place a non-stick pan over medium heat, and add the olive oil to heat. Then add the butter, brown sugar, and maple syrup. Allow the sugar and the maple syrup to dissolve before adding the oats and walnut to the pan. Mix all the content together until the dry Ingredients: are well coated.
4. Evenly spread the mixture to the lined baking tray and place the tray in the oven to bake for approximately twenty minutes.
5. Set the granola aside for some minutes to cool, then break it up, add the chocolate chips, then mix them all together. Serve immediately or store in a jar for up to ten days.

Buckwheat with Coconut and Nuts

Ingredients:

- Buckwheat flakes 1 cup
- Buckwheat puffs 1 cup
- Cocoa nibs 5 tablespoons
- Coconut flakes 4 tablespoons
- Chopped strawberries 2 cup
- Medjool dates ½ cup
- Greek or soy yogurt 1 cup
- Walnut two and a 1 tablespoon

Directions:
1. Mix all the Ingredients: in a serving bowl and enjoy!

2. Alternatively, you may mix all the dry Ingredients: and store in a glass jar or container. Add the yogurt before you serve.

Simple Celery Juice

Ingredients:

- 2 lemon, peeled
- ½ cup of filtered water
- Eight celery stalks with leaves
- 2 tbsp fresh ginger, peeled
- Pinch of salt

Directions:

1. Put all the Ingredients: inside the blender, pulse until well combined.
2. Through a fine-mesh strainer, strain the juice and transfer it into two glasses.
3. Serve immediately.

Kale, Apple, and Celery Juice

Ingredients:

- 1/2 apple with skin
- 1/2 organic lemon with peel
- 1-inch piece of ginger with peel
- Ten celery stalks with leaves
- 2 medium cucumber
- A handful of kale stems removes

Directions:

1. Wash all Ingredients: well and cut them to fit the feed chute of the juicer.
2. Then gradually pour into the feed chute and allow pressing out. If you prepare more juice in stock, the juice will last 2 or two days in the refrigerator.

Citrus Fruit Salad

Ingredients:

For Salad:

- 1 grapefruit, peeled and segmented
- 2 tablespoons unsweetened dried cranberries
- 3 cups fresh kale, tough ribs removed and torn
- 1 orange, peeled and segmented

For Dressing:

- ½ teaspoon raw h2y
- Salt and ground black pepper, as required
- 2 tablespoons extra-virgin olive oil
- 2 tablespoons fresh orange juice
- 1 teaspoon Dijon mustard

Directions:

1. For salad: in a salad bowl, place all Ingredients: and mix.
2. For dressing: place all Ingredients: in another bowl and beat until well combined.
3. Place dressing on top of salad and toss to coat well. Serve immediately.

Mixed Berries Salad

Ingredients:

- ½ cup fresh raspberries
- 6 cups fresh arugula
- 2 tablespoons extra-virgin olive oil
- 1 cup fresh strawberries, hulled and sliced
- ½ cup fresh blackberries
- ½ cup fresh blueberries
- Salt and ground black pepper, as required

Directions:
1. In a salad bowl, place all the Ingredients: and toss to coat well.
2. Serve immediately.

Shakshuka oriental vegetable stew with eggs

Ingredients:

- 600 g chunky tomatoes (can)
- 1 tsp cumin
- 1 pinch cayenne pepper (or chilli powder)
- salt
- 8 eggs
- ½ fret parsley
- 1 onion
- 1 red chilli pepper
- 1 bell pepper
- 3 tbsp olive oil
- 2 tbsp tomato paste

- 250 g wholemeal flatbread

Directions:

1. Peel and slice the onion into strips. The chilli and the peppers are cleaned, washed, halved and removed and the chilli is cut into small pieces and the peppers into cubes.
2. In a saucepan, heat the olive oil, fry the onions, chilli and paprika over medium heat until they are translucent.
3. Add the tomato paste and fry for 2 minutes, then add the tomatoes and deglaze. For about 10 minutes, season with cumin, cayenne pepper and salt and simmer.
4. In 4 ovenproof moulds, pour the contents of the pan, use a spoon to make two hollows in the sauce and let 2 cracked egg slide into each.
5. Bake the Shakshuka for about 8-10 minutes in a preheated oven at 200 ° C (convection 180 ° C; gas: level 3) until the eggs are set.

6. Meanwhile, wash the parsley, shake it dry and chop it roughly. Sprinkle with parsley and serve with flatbread. Take the Shakshuka out of the oven.

Vegetable and lentil stew with peas

Ingredients:

- ½ tsp curry powder

- 600 ml vegetable broth

- salt

- pepper

- 4 tbsp coconut milk

- 2 pieces spring onions

- 150 g frozen pea

- 2 tsp sunflower seeds

- 5 g ginger tuber

- 1 shallot

- 1 sweet potato

- 100 g celery root

- 2 tbsp olive oil

- 80 g red lenses

- 1 tsp harissa paste

- 1 tbsp tomato paste

Directions:

1. Peel and chop the ginger and shallot. Clean and peel the sweet potato and celery and cut into small cubes.
2. Heat 1 tablespoon of oil in a saucepan, sauté the ginger, shallot, sweet potato and celery over medium heat for 5 minutes. Add the lentils, harissa, tomato paste and curry powder and cook for 4 minutes.
3. Pour the vegetable stock, season with salt and pepper and let the soup simmer for about 15 minutes. Then stir in 2 tablespoons of coconut milk.
4. At the same time, clean, wash and chop the spring onions. Heat the remaining oil in a pan, fry the onion, peas and sunflower seeds for 5 minutes.
5. Fill the soup into two bowls, drizzle with the remaining coconut milk and top with the peas.

Strawberry buckwheat tabouleh

Ingredients:

- 25g Medjool dates, pitted
- 1 tbsp capers
- 30g parsley
- 100g strawberries, hulled
- 1 tbsp extra virgin olive oil
- juce of ½ lemon
- 50g buckwheat
- 1 tbsp ground turmeric 80g avocado
- 65g tomato
- 20g red onion
- 30g rocket

Directions:

1. Cook the buckwheat with the turmeric according to the packet instructions. Drain and keep to 2 side to cool.
2. Finely chop the avocado, tomato, red onion, dates, capers and parsley and mix with the cool buckwheat.
3. Slice the strawberries and gently mix into the salad with the oil and lemon juice. Serve on a bed of rocket.

Sirtfood Bites

Ingredients:

- 1 cup (120g) walnuts

- 1 ounce (30g) dark chocolate (85 percent cocoa solids), broken into pieces; or 1/4 cup cocoa nibs

- 9 ounces (250g) Medjool dates, pitted

- 1 tablespoon cocoa powder

- 1 tablespoon ground turmeric

- 1 tablespoon extra virgin olive oil

- the scraped seeds of 1 vanilla pod or 1 teaspoon vanilla extract

- 1 to 2 tablespoons water

Directions:

1. Place the walnuts and chocolate in a food processor and process until you have a fine powder.
2. Add all the other ingredients except the water and blend until the mixture forms a ball. You may or may not have to add the water depending on the consistency of the mixture— you don't want it to be too sticky.

3. Using your hands, form the mixture into bitesize balls and refrigerate in an airtight container for at least 1 hour before eating them.
4. You could roll some of the balls in some more cocoa or dried coconut to achieve a different finish if you like. They will keep for up to 1 week in your fridge.

Chocolate Cupcakes with Matcha Icing

Ingredients::

- ½ tsp fine espresso coffee, decaf if preferred
- 120ml milk
- ½ tsp vanilla extract
- 50ml vegetable oil
- 1 egg
- 120ml boiling water
- 150g self-raising flour
- 200g caster sugar
- 60g cocoa
- ½ tsp salt

For the icing:

- ½ tsp vanilla bean paste

- 50g soft cream cheese

- 50g butter, at room temperature

- 50g icing sugar

- 1 tbsp matcha green tea powder

Directions:

1. Preheat the oven to 180C/160C fan. Line a cupcake tin with paper or silicone cake cases.
2. Place the flour, sugar, cocoa, salt and espresso powder in a large bowl and mix thoroughly.
3. Add the milk, vanilla extract, vegetable oil and egg to the dry Ingredients:and use an electric mixer to beat until 54 well combined.
4. Carefully pour in the boiling water slowly and beat on a low speed until fully combined. Use a high speed to beat for a further minute to add air to the batter.
5. The batter is much more liquid than a normal cake mix. Have faith, it will taste amazing!
6. Spoon the batter evenly between the cake cases. Each cake case should be no more than ¾ full.
7. Bake in the oven for 15-18 minutes, until the mixture bounces back when tapped. Remove

from the oven and allow to cool completely before icing.

8. To make the icing, cream the butter and icing sugar together until it's pale and smooth. Add the matcha powder and vanilla and stir again.

9. Finally add the cream cheese and beat until smooth. Pipe or spread over the cakes.

Sesame Chicken Salad

Ingredients::

- ½ red onion, very finely sliced
- Large handful 20g parsley, chopped
- 150g cooked chicken, shredded
- 1 tbsp sesame seeds
- 1 cucumber, peeled, halved lengthways, deseeded with a teaspoon and sliced
- 100g baby kale, roughly chopped
- 60g pak choi, very finely shredded

For the dressing:

- 1 tsp clear honey
- 2 tsp soy sauce

- 1 tbsp extra virgin olive oil

- 1 tsp sesame oil

- Juice of 1 lime

Directions:

1. Toast the sesame seeds in a dry frying pan for 2 minutes until lightly browned and fragrant. Transfer to a plate to cool.
2. In a small bowl, mix together the olive oil, sesame oil, lime juice, h2y and soy sauce to make the dressing.
3. Place the cucumber, kale, pak choi, red onion and parsley in a large bowl and gently mix together. Pour over the dressing and mix again.
4. Distribute the salad between two plates and top with the shredded chicken. Sprinkle over the sesame seeds just before serving.

Lamb, Butternut Squash And Date Tagine Sirtfood Recipes

Ingredients:

- ½ teaspoon salt

- 100g medjool dates, pitted and chopped

- 400g tin chopped tomatoes, plus half a can of water

- 500g butternut squash, chopped into 1cm cubes

- 400g tin chickpeas, drained

- 2 tablespoons fresh coriander plus extra for garnish

- 2 tablespoons olive oil

- 1 red onion, sliced

- 2cm ginger, grated

- 3 garlic cloves, grated or crushed

- 1 teaspoon chilli flakes or to taste

- 2 teaspoons cumin seeds

- 1 cinnamon stick

- 2 teaspoons ground turmeric

- 800g lamb neck fillet, cut into 2cm chunks

- Buckwheat, couscous, flatbreads or rice to serve

Directions:

1. Preheat your oven to 140C.
2. Drizzle about 2 tablespoons of olive oil into a large ovenproof saucepan or cast iron casserole dish.
3. Add the sliced onion and cook on a gentle heat, with the lid on, for about 5 minutes, until the onions are softened but not brown.
4. Add the grated garlic and ginger, chilli, cumin, cinnamon and turmeric.
5. Stir well and cook for 1 more minute with the lid off. Add a splash of water if it gets too dry.
6. Next add in the lamb chunks. Stir well to coat the meat in the onions and spices and then add the salt, chopped dates and tomatoes, plus about 1 a can of water 100-200ml.
7. Bring the tagine to the boil and then put the lid on and put in your preheated oven for 1 hour and 15 minutes.

8. Thirty minutes before the end of the cooking time, add in the chopped butternut squash and drained chickpeas.
9. Stir everything together, put the lid back on and return to the oven for the final 30 minutes of cooking.
10. When the tagine is ready, remove from the oven and stir through the chopped coriander. Serve with buckwheat, couscous, flatbreads or basmati rice.

Prawn Arrabbiata-Sirtfood Recipes

Ingredients::

- 1 Bird's eye chilli, finely chopped

- 1 tsp Dried mixed herbs

- 1 tsp Extra virgin olive oil

- 2 tbsp White wine optional

- 400 g Tinned chopped tomatoes

- 125-150 g Raw or cooked prawns Ideally king prawns

- 65 g Buckwheat pasta

- 1 tbsp Extra virgin olive oil

- For arrabbiata sauce

- 40 g Red onion, finely chopped

- 1 Garlic clove, finely chopped 30 g Celery, finely chopped

- 1 tbsp Chopped parsley

Directions:
1. Fry the onion, garlic, celery and chilli and dried herbs in the oil over a mediumlow heat for 1 2 minutes.
2. Turn the heat up to medium, add the wine and cook for 1 minute.
3. Add the tomatoes and leave the sauce to simmer over a mediumlow heat for 2030 minutes, until it has a nice rich consistency. If you feel the sauce is getting too thick simply add a little water.
4. While the sauce is cooking bring a pan of water to the boil and cook the pasta according to the packet Directions:.
5. When cooked to your liking, drain, toss with the olive oil and keep in the pan until needed.

6. If you are using raw prawns add them to the sauce and cook for a further 34 minutes, until they have turned pink and opaque, add the parsley and serve.
7. If you are using cooked prawns add them with the parsley, bring the sauce to the boil and serve.
8. Add the cooked pasta to the sauce, mix thoroughly but gently and serve.

Baked Salmon Salad With Creamy Mint Dressing

Ingredients:

- 50g of cucumber cut into chunks

- 3 spring onions trimmed & sliced

- 2 small handful of parsley roughly chopped

- 2 salmon fillet

- 40grams of mixed salad leaves

- 40grams of young spinach leaves

- 3 radishes trimmed & thinly sliced

For the dressing:

- 3 leaves mint finely chopped

- Salt

- Freshly ground black pepper

- 2 teaspoon of low-fat mayonnaise

- 2 tablespoon of natural yogurt

- 2 tablespoon of rice vinegar

Directions:

1. Firstly you should heat up the oven to 200 degrees Celsius.
2. Place the salmon fillet on a clean baking tray and then bake for about sixteen to eighteen mins.
3. The salmon goes well in the salad either hot or cold. Salmon with skin will require you cook with skin side down.
4. A fish slice can be used to remove the salmon skin after cooking. It should slide off easily when cooked.
5. In a clean small container, mix together the yogurt, rice wine vinegar, mint leaves, salt, pepper and mayonnaise together and let it

stand for a minimum of five minutes to allow the flavors get deeper.
6. Place the spinach and salad leaves on a dishing plate and then top with the cucumber, parsley, spring onions and radishes.
7. Gently flake the cooked salmon onto the salad and then drizzle the dressing over to enjoy.

Choc Chip Granola

Ingredients:

- 4 tablespoons of light olive oil
- 2 tablespoon of dark brown sugar
- 20grams of butter
- 3 tablespoons of rice malt syrup
- 50grams of pecans roughly chopped
- 200grams of jumbo oats
- 60grams dark chocolate chips

Directions:

1. Heat up the oven to 160 degrees Fahrenheit. Line a clean large baking tray with a silic2 sheet or baking parchment.
2. Mix the pecans and oats together in a clean big container. In a clean small non-stick pan,

gently heat the butter, olive oil, rice malt syrup and brown sugar until the butter is melted and the syrup and sugar have also dissolved. Ensure not to allow it boil.
3. Afterwards, pour the syrup over the oats and vigorously stir until the oats are fully covered.
4. Arrange the granola over the baking tray, arranging in the corners. Now leave clumps of mixture with spacing rather than an uniform spread.
5. Bake in the oven for twenty mins until it appears tinged golden brown at the edges.
6. Take out from the oven and then leave on tray to let cool completely.
7. When it gets cool, using your fingers, ensure there aren't any bigger lumps on the tray and having d2 that mix in the chocolate chips.
8. Scoop the granola into an airtight jar. You can store granola for a minimum of 3 weeks.

Bumper oat cookies

Ingredients:

- ½ tsp bicarbonate of soda
- 250g porridge oats
- 1 tsp ground cinnamon
- 100g each of ready-to-eat dried apricots, chopped and stem ginger , chopped
- 75-80g pack dried sour cherries
- 2 tbsp boiling water
- 175g butter
- 175g demerara sugar
- 100g golden syrup
- 85g plain flour
- 1 medium egg , beaten

Directions:
1. Heat the oven to 180C/fan160C/gas 4. Line several baking sheets with baking parchment or non-stick sheets.
2. Warm the butter, sugar and golden syrup in a large saucepan over a medium heat until the butter has melted.
3. Stir in the flour, bicarbonate of soda, oats, cinnamon, dried fruits and ginger, then the water and finally the egg. Leave to cool until easy to handle.
4. With dampened hands, shape the mixture into 18 large balls, then flatten them onto the baking sheets allowing plenty of space for spreading and bake for 15-20 mins until golden. (This will give a soft, chewy cookie. For a crisper 2, reduce the heat to 160C/fan140C/gas 3 and bake for a further 5-10 mins.)

5. Allow the cookies to cool on the trays briefly, then lift onto to a cooling rack. Will keep in an airtight container, separated with baking parchment, for up to 1 week.

Roast tomatoes with asparagus & black olives

Ingredients:

- extra-virgin olive oil
- 6 garlic cloves , peeled and halved
- 24 asparagus spears
- 750g cherry tomatoes
- a handful of black olives , st2d and chopped

Directions:

1. Preheat the oven to fan 180C/conventional 200C/gas 6. Spread the tomatoes out on a large baking tray and prick each 2 with a fork.
2. Sprinkle with olive oil, sea salt and freshly ground black pepper and scatter with the garlic. Roast in the oven for 15 minutes.
3. Lay asparagus flat in a large frying pan over a medium heat.

4. Splash with 3 tbsp olive oil, sprinkle with sea salt and freshly ground black pepper. Roll the spears until they're hot and evenly coated with oil.
5. Remove tomatoes from oven and pour off the excess juice.
6. Push tomatoes to 2 side of tray and lay asparagus next to them. Return to oven and roast for 15 minutes.
7. Sprinkle with the olives before serving warm or at room temperature.
8. Vegetables can be done up to two hours before serving and kept at room temperature.

Stuffed peppers with buckwheat

Ingredients:

- 1 teaspoon paprika powder
- 1 teaspoon basil
- 1 lemon, juice of it
- 1 teaspoon of salt
- 1 teaspoon pepper
- 1 teaspoon olive oil
- 1 teaspoon chilli flakes
- 1 teaspoon of coarse salt
- 1 teaspoon fresh coriander
- 4 peppers
- 100g buckwheat

- 175g chickpea and avocado spread

- 2 carrots

- 1 red pepper

- 80ml water

- 1 teaspoon garlic powder

Directions:

1. Before we start, let's preheat the oven to 180 ° C.
2. Bake the pitted 1 peppers in a baking pan in the oven for 15 to 20 minutes. Pour a little olive oil over it.
3. Meanwhile, cook the buckwheat in a saucepan with water for 15 minutes.
4. We need the red peppers and carrots in small cubes. Mix this with the finished buckwheat, the spread, garlic powder, paprika powder, basil, lemon juice, salt and pepper in a bowl.

5. Fill the baked 1 peppers with the filling and bake in the oven for another 5-8 minutes.
6. Season everything with a little chilli flakes, salt and coriander and serve.

Blueberry salad with crispy tempeh strips

Ingredients:

for the salad:

- 200g tempeh
- 1 tbsp coconut oil
- 1 tbsp soy sauce
- 150g blueberries
- 300g radicchio
- 1 romaine lettuce

For the dressing:

- 2 tbsp lemon juice
- 0.5 tsp salt
- 0.5 tsp black pepper

- 0.5 tsp cinnamon

- 150g blueberries

- 50ml dark balsamic vinegar

- 2 tbsp olive oil

Directions:

1. For the salad, the radicchio and the romaine, cut in 1 and cut off the stalk. Cut the leaves into fine strips and place in a bowl with the blueberries.
2. Now prepare the dressing. To do this, put all the Ingredients: in a bowl and puree.
3. Heat the coconut oil in a pan. Cut the tempeh into slices and fry. Deglaze with the soy sauce.
4. Pour the dressing over the salad and serve with the tempeh strips.

GRILLED LEEKS WITH POMEGRANATE VINAIGRETTE

Ingredients:

For the pomegranate vinaigrette

- 1/2 teaspoon Dijon mustard

- 1 shallot, minced

- 1/4 teaspoon coarse salt

- 1/8 teaspoon freshly ground black pepper

- 1 pomegranate

- 1 tablespoon raspberry vinegar

- 1/3 cup   extra virgin olive oil

For the leeks

- 1/8 teaspoon ground black pepper

- 1 tablespoon pine nuts, lightly toasted

- 1 tablespoon chopped fresh mint or flat-leaf parsley

- 4 leeks, trimmed

- 2 tablespoons extra virgin olive oil

- 1/4 teaspoon coarse salt

Directions:

For the pomegranate vinaigrette

1. Cut the pomegranate in half from stem to blossom end. Reserve half of the pomegranate for another use.
2. Cut the other half in half again from stem to blossom end. Remove all of the seeds and transfer half of the seeds to a minichopper or food processor, reserving the remaining seeds.
3. Process until the juice and seeds separate, and then strain the juice into a cup or bowl.
4. Measure out 3 tablespoons pomegranate juice and transfer to a small bowl.
5. Add the vinegar and then whisk in the extra virgin olive oil in a steady stream until blended. Whisk in the mustard, shallot, salt, and pepper.

For the leeks

6. Light a grill for direct medium-high heat, about 400ºf.
7. Trim off the tough green tops and the roots of the leeks, and then halve the leeks lengthwise.
8. Rinse the cut sides under cold running water to remove any grit from between the layers. Pat dry and rub all over with the extra virgin olive oil.
9. Season all over with the salt and pepper. Brush the grill grate and coat with oil. Grill the leeks, cut side down, until nicely grill-marked, 3 to 4 minutes. Flip and grill until just tender, about 3 minutes more. Transfer to a platter and top with the vinaigrette, pine nuts, reserved pomegranate seeds, and mint.

TATTOOED POTATOES WITH ROSEMARY

Ingredients:

- 6 small fresh rosemary sprigs or Italian parsley leaves
- 3 russet potatoes, unpeeled, cut in half lengthwise
- 1/3 to ½ cup extra virgin olive oil
- 1 tsp. salt
- ½ tsp. freshly cracked pepper

Directions:

1. Preheat an oven to 400 degrees F.
2. Pour extra virgin olive oil into a medium-sized glass baking dish; add salt and pepper. Stir to combine.
3. Press a rosemary sprig or parsley leaf on the cut side of each potato half and place cut side

down in the oil. Bake until the potatoes are nicely browned, 40 to 45 minutes.
4. While the potatoes are cooking, using a spatula, gently move them every now and then to keep them from sticking.
5. When they are ready, remove them for the pan, turning them flat side up and carefully leaving the pressed herb in place. Arrange on a platter and serve immediately.

Salad Smoothie

Ingredients:

- 2 tablespoons parsley
- 2 tablespoons lemon juice
- 1 cup crushed ice
- 1 cup arugula
- ½ cucumber
- 1/2 small red onion
- 1 tablespoon olive oil or cumin oil

Directions:

1. Put all the Ingredients: into a blender with some water and blitz until smooth. Add ice to make your smoothie refreshing.

Avocado Kale Smoothie

Ingredients:

- 1 celery stalk
- 1 tablespoon chia seeds
- 1 cup crushed ice
- 1 cup kale
- ½ avocado
- 1 cup cucumber
- 1 tablespoon spirulina

Directions:

1. Place all the Ingredients: into a blender and add in enough water to cover them. Process until smooth, serve and enjoy.

Prawn Stir Fry

Ingredients:

- 4 cloves of garlic

- 4 bird's eye chili (less to taste or cut out the seeds to taste if you prefer it less spicy)

- 4 teaspoons fresh, minced ginger

- 2/3 cup of red onion, diced

- 1 1/3 cup celery, chopped

- 2 cups of green beans, chopped

- 3 cups of kale, chopped

- 4 cups of raw shelled prawns, larger in size preferred, but any size will be fine

- 8 tablespoons soy sauce

- 8 tablespoons olive oil

- 10 ounces of buckwheat noodles

- 2 cups of chicken stock

Directions:
1. Heat up a frying pan on high heat. Add the prawns with 4 teaspoons of soy sauce and 4 teaspoons of olive oil.
2. Cook for 3 minutes and move prawns to a plate. Clean the pan with paper towels and set aside.
3. Prepare your noodles according to the packaging. Drain and set aside.
4. Add remaining oil to the frying pan and add in all of your vegetables. Cook at medium-high for 2-3 minutes and then add the stock.
5. Bring to a boil, then drop the temperature and allow it to simmer for two minutes. Then, add the prawns and the noodles. Bring back to a boil to warm them up and remove from heat.

Chicken Zucchini Stir Fry

Ingredients:

- 1 tablespoons olive oil
- 1 tablespoon garlic, minced
- 1 tablespoon ginger, minced
- 1 pound thinly sliced chicken breast
- 2 cups zucchini, sliced in thin 1-circles
- ¼ cup of soy sauce
- 1 cup of broth (chicken or veggie)
- 1 tablespoon corn starch
- 2 tablespoons (Japanese sweet white wine)
- 1 tablespoons h2y
- 2 teaspoons sesame oil

- Green onions for garnish

Directions:
1. Add your soy sauce, broth, mirin, h2y, sesame oil, and corn starch into a bowl and whisk thoroughly until well combined
2. Take a large frying pan or wok and add a teaspoon of olive oil on medium-high heat. Cook 1 of the chicken in 2 flat layer until cooked through—2-3 minutes per side.
3. Then, set aside and repeat with the remaining 1 of chicken and another 1 teaspoon of oil.
4. Add in the last teaspoon of oil and the ginger and garlic. Cook until fragrant—roughly 1 of a minute.
5. Then, stir in the sauce that you prepared in a bowl. Whisk well and cook for a minute. It should start to warm up and thicken.
6. Add zucchini and cook another two minutes until the zucchini is tender-crisp. Remove from heat and mix the prepared chicken into

the mixture, coating well. Serve with green onions on top.

Sirtfood Lentil Soup

Ingredients:

- 3 garlic cloves, minced
- 2 carrots, chopped
- 2 celery stalks, chopped
- 6 cups vegetable broth
- 1 teaspoon dried thyme
- 1 bay leaf
- 4 cups chopped kale
- 1 cup brown or green lentils, rinsed and drained
- 1 tablespoon olive oil
- 1 onion, chopped

- Salt and pepper to taste

Drections:

1. In a large pot or Dutch oven, heat the olive oil over medium heat. Add the onion and garlic and sauté until the onion is translucent, about 5 minutes.
2. Add the chopped carrots and celery to the pot and sauté for another 5-7 minutes, until the vegetables have softened.
3. Add the rinsed and drained lentils to the pot and stir to combine.
4. Pour in the vegetable broth, thyme, and bay leaf. Bring the mixture to a boil, then reduce the heat and let it simmer for 30-40 minutes, or until the lentils are tender.
5. In the last 10 minutes of cooking, stir in the chopped kale and continue to simmer until the kale is wilted and tender.
6. Remove the bay leaf and season the soup with salt and pepper to taste.

7. Serve the lentil soup hot with a side of crusty bread, if desired.

Grilled Steak with Roasted Vegetables

Ingredients:

- 1 cup Brussels sprouts, trimmed and halved
- 1 large sweet potato, peeled and chopped into small cubes
- 2 garlic cloves, minced
- 1 teaspoon dried thyme
- 1/2 teaspoon paprika
- 1 lb steak (such as sirloin, ribeye, or flank)
- Salt and pepper to taste
- 2 tablespoons olive oil
- 2 cups broccoli florets
- 1/4 teaspoon cumin

Drections:

1. Preheat your grill to medium-high heat.
2. Season the steak with salt and pepper on both sides. Brush with 1 tablespoon of olive oil.
3. Grill the steak for 4-5 minutes per side for medium-rare, or until it reaches your desired level of d2ness. Remove the steak from the grill and let it rest for 5-10 minutes before slicing.
4. In the meantime, preheat your oven to 400°F (200°C). Line a baking sheet with parchment paper.
5. In a large bowl, toss the broccoli florets, Brussels sprouts, and sweet potato with the remaining tablespoon of olive oil, minced garlic, dried thyme, paprika, cumin, salt, and pepper.
6. Spread the vegetables in a single layer on the prepared baking sheet. Roast in the oven for

25-30 minutes, or until they are tender and golden brown.
7. Serve the grilled steak with the roasted vegetables on the side.
8. Enjoy!

Miso-Marinated Baked Cod with Stir-Fried Greens & Sesame

Ingredients:

- 2 teaspoon of fresh ginger (finely chopped)
- 3/8 cup of green beans
- 1/4 cup of buckwheat
- 2 teaspoon of sesame seeds
- Two tablespoons of parsley (roughly chopped)
- 2 teaspoons of ground turmeric
- 2 tablespoon of tamari (or soy sauce, for gluten-free)
- 3/4 cup of kale (roughly chopped)
- 2 tablespoon of mirin
- 4 and a 1 teaspoons of miso

- 1 by 7-ounce skinless cod fillet

- 1/8 cup of red onion (sliced)

- 3/8 cup of celery (sliced)

- 2 tablespoon of extra-virgin olive oil

- Two garlic cloves (finely chopped)

- 2 Thai chili (finely chopped)

Directions:

1. Preheat the oven to 425 degrees Fahrenheit. Mix the mirin, 2 teaspoon of the oil and miso. Rub all the cod and leave for about 30 mins to marinate.
2. After you've d2 that, bake the cod for approximately 10 mins.
3. Heat up a big frying pan or wok with the rest of the oil. You should then add the onion and stir-fry for some mins, then add the garlic, kale, chili, green beans, ginger, and celery.
4. Toss and fry until the kale becomes tender and well cooked through. You will have to add some water to the pan to support the process of cooking.
5. Cook the buckwheat together with the turmeric (according to package Directions:).
6. Add the parsley, tamari and sesame seeds to the stir-fry and then serve with fish and buckwheat.

Prawn Arrabbiata

Ingredients:

- 125grams raw or cooked prawns
- 65grams Buckwheat pasta
- 2 tablespoon of extra virgin olive oil

For Arrabbiata Sauce:

- 2 teaspoon of Extra virgin olive oil
- 400grams Tinned chopped tomatoes
- 2 teaspoon of Dried mixed herbs
- 2 tablespoon of Chopped parsley
- 2 Garlic clove (finely chopped)
- 40grams Red onion (finely chopped)
- 30grams Celery (finely chopped)

- 2 Bird's eye chilli (finely chopped)

- Two tablespoon of White wine (if desired)

Directions:
1. Fry the garlic, onion, chili, celery and also the dried herbs in the oil over a medium to low heat for 2 to two minutes.
2. Increase the heat up to medium, and then add the wine and cook for 2 minute.
3. Having d2 that, add the tomatoes and then leave the sauce to simmer over a medium to low heat for twenty to thirty minutes, until it has a lovely consistency.
4. You can some water if the sauce is too thick.
5. Just as the sauce is cooking bring a pan of water to the boil and then cook the pasta following to the packet Directions:.
6. After you've cooked it as desired, drain, toss with the olive oil and then leave in the pan until it will be required.

7. If using raw prawns, add them to the sauce and cook for a further 4 to 5 mins, until they have turned pink and also opaque, add the parsley and then serve. If using cooked prawns add them with the parsley, bring the sauce to the boil and serve.
8. Add the pasta (cooketo the sauce, mix but carefully and then serve.

Mixed Berry Yogurt

Ingredients:

- 85% cocoa dark chocolate 10g

- Chopped walnut 25g

- Mixed berries 1 cup

- Greek yogurt 1 cup

Directions:

1. Add all the Ingredients: into a serving bowl, mix together, and serve immediately.

Salsa Bean Dip

Ingredients:

- Low-fat cheddar 2 cup
- Salsa 1 cup
- Chopped green onions two tablespoons
- Canned white beans two cups (drain and rinse, do not add salt)

Directions:

1. Place a small pot over medium heat, add the salsa, green onions, and beans into the pot, stir together and bring to a simmer.
2. Then cook for approximately twenty minutes before you add the cheese.
3. Stir the food until the cheese melts, put off the heat, and set the pot aside to cool.
4. Enjoy!

Creamy Sunshine Smoothie

Ingredients:

- 5 leaves of kale, destemmed
- ½ cup of pineapple juice
- 8 oz. of coconut water
- 1 avocado, pitted and scooped out
- 1 banana

Directions:

1. Place the liquids, then the fruits and veggies into a blender and blend until smooth.
2. Serve immediately or slightly chilled.

Blueberries and Coconut Smoothie

Ingredients:

- 1 ½ cup of almond milk
- ½ tsp of ground cinnamon
- 2 tbsp of coconut flakes
- 3 mint leaves
- 1 banana, peeled and cut
- 2 dry Medjool dates, without seeds
- 1 tsp coconut oil
- ½ cup of blueberries

Directions:
1. Put all of the Ingredients: listed above in a blender and blend thoroughly.
2. Serve immediately or slightly chilled.

3. For an extra kick, decorate with coconut flakes and mint leaves.

Butternut Pumpkin with Buckwheat

Ingredients:

- 300ml vegetable broth
- 100g dates, seeded and chopped
- 2 400g tin of chick peas, drained
- 500g butter squash, peeled, seeded and cut into pieces
- 200g buckwheat
- 5g coriander, chopped
- 10g parsley, chopped
- 1 tablespoon of extra virgin olive oil
- 1 red onion, finely chopped
- 1 tablespoon fresh ginger, finely chopped

- 3 cloves of garlic, finely chopped
- 2 small chilies, finely chopped
- 1 tablespoon cumin
- 1 cinnamon stick
- 2 tablespoons turmeric
- 800g chopped canned tomatoes

Directions:
1. Preheat oven to 400 °. Heat the olive oil in a frying pan and sauté the onion, ginger, garlic and Tai chili.
2. After two minutes add cumin, cinnamon and turmeric and cook for another two minutes while stirring.
3. Add the tomatoes, dates, stock and chickpeas, stir well and cook over a low heat for 45 to 60 minutes. Add some water as required.

4. In the meantime, mix the pumpkin pieces with olive oil and bake in the oven for about 30 minutes until soft.
5. Cook the buckwheat according to the Directions:and add the remaining turmeric.
6. When everything is cooked, add the pumpkin to the other Ingredients: in the roaster and serve with the buckwheat. Sprinkle with coriander and parsley.

Chicken and Kale with Spicy Salsa

Ingredients:

- 1 tbsp. extra virgin olive oil
- 1 cup kale, chopped
- 1/2 red onion, sliced
- 1 skinless, b2less chicken filet/breast
- ¼ cup buckwheat
- 1/4 lemon, juiced

Salsa:

- Juice of 1/4 lemon
- 1 tsp. fresh ginger, chopped
- 2 tsp. ground turmeric
- 1 tomato

- 3 sprigs of parsley, chopped

- 1 tbsp. chopped capers

- 1 chili, deseeded and minced

Directions:

1. Chop all Ingredients: above, just for the salsa, and set aside in a bowl. Pre-eat the oven to 425 F.
2. Add a teaspoon of the turmeric, the lemon juice and a little oil to the chicken, cover and set aside for 10 minutes.
3. In a hot pan, slide the chicken and marinade and cook for 2-3 minutes each side, on high to sear it.
4. Then, slide it all onto a baking-safe dish and for cook for about 20 minutes or until cooked.
5. Lightly steam the kale in a steamer, or on the stovetop with a lid and some water, for about 5 minutes. You want to wilt the kale, not boil or burn it.

6. Sautee the red onions and ginger, and after 4-5 minutes, add the cooked kale and stir for 1 minute.
7. Cook the buckwheat, adding in the turmeric see package or look online if it was bought in bulk.
8. Serve the chicken along with the buckwheat, kale, and spicy salsa.

Cottage cheese with fruit

Ingredients:

- 1 kiwi
- ½ mango
- 75 g strawberries
- 400 g cottage cheese
- 30 g almonds
- 1 orange
- 1 tbsp h2y

Directions:

1. Roast the almonds in a pan without fat over medium heat for 3-4 minutes and let them cool.

2. Squeeze 1 orange. Fillet the other orange. Peel the kiwi and mango. Cut the mango pulp at the core and dice both.
3. Wash, clean and quarter the strawberries. Mix the cut fruit with orange juice in a bowl.
4. Mix the cottage cheese with h2y and divide into two bowls. Pour the fruit salad on top, sprinkle with roasted almonds and serve.

Tea-Cake

Ingredients:

- 50 ml lukewarm milk (3.5% fat)
- 80 g room temperature butter
- 1 egg
- 50 g almond flour (partially de-oiled)
- 1 tsp organic lemon peel
- ¼ tsp vanilla powder
- 1 pinch salt
- 250 g low-fat quark
- 150 g raisins
- 4 tbsp orange juice
- 450 g spelled flour type 1050

- 30 g fresh yeast

- 60 g raw cane sugar

- 1 egg yolk

Directions:

1. Drizzle the raisins with orange juice and set aside.
2. Sift the flour into a large bowl, making a well in the middle. Put the yeast with 1 teaspoon of sugar and milk in the well and dust with a little flour from the edge. Cover the pre-dough and let rise for about 10 minutes.
3. Add the remaining sugar, pieces of butter, egg, almond flour, lemon peel, vanilla, salt and low-fat quark to the pre-dough. Use the dough hook of a hand mixer to work all Ingredients: into a smooth dough. Cover with a damp tea towel and let rise at room temperature for about 1 hour.

4. Line a baking sheet with parchment paper. Briefly knead the raisins into the yeast dough.
5. Divide the yeast dough into 10 portions, shape into balls and place on the baking sheet with a gap. Whisk the egg yolk with 1 tbsp water and brush the raisin rolls with it.
6. Bake the raisin rolls in a preheated oven at 200 ° C (convection 180 ° C; gas: level 3) for 2025 minutes until golden brown.
7. Take out the raisin rolls and let them cool on a wire rack. Enjoy lukewarm or cold.

Choc Chip Granola

Ingredients:

- 20g butter
- 1 tbsp dark brown sugar
- 2 tbsp rice malt syrup
- 200g jumbo oats
- 50g pecans, roughly Chopped
- 3 tbsp light olive oil
- 60g good-quality (70%) Dark chocolate chips

Directions:

1. Preheat the oven to 160°C (140°C fan/Gas 3). Line a large baking tray with a silicone sheet or baking parchment.

2. Mix the oats and pecans together in a large bowl. In a small non-stick pan, gently heat the olive oil, butter, brown sugar and rice malt syrup until the butter has melted and the sugar and syrup have dissolved.
3. Do not allow to boil. Pour the syrup over the oats and stir thoroughly until the oats are fully covered.
4. Distribute the granola over the baking tray, spreading right into the corners. Leave clumps of mixture with spacing rather than an even spread. Bake in the oven for 20 minutes until just tinged golden brown at the edges.
5. Remove from the oven and leave to cool on the tray completely.
6. When cool, break up any bigger lumps on the tray with your fingers and then mix in the chocolate chips.

7. Scoop or pour the granola into an airtight tub or jar. The granola will keep for at least 2 weeks.

Strawberries Cream

Ingredients:

- Zest of 1 lemon, grated
- ½ C. Heavy cream
- 3 egg yolks, whisked
- ½ c. stevia
- 2 lbs. Strawberries, chopped
- 1 c. Almond milk

Directions:

1. Heat up a pan with the milk over medium-high heat, add the stevia and the rest of the Ingredients:, whisk well, simmer for 20 minutes, divide into cups and serve cold.

Apples and Plum Cake

Ingredients:

- 2 lbs. Plums, pitted and cut into quarters
- 2 apples, cored and chopped
- Zest of 1 lemon, grated
- 1 tsp. baking powder
- 7 oz. almond flour
- 1 egg, whisked 5 tablespoons stevia
- 3 oz. Warm almond milk

Directions:

1. In a bowl, mix the almond milk with the egg, stevia, and the rest of the Ingredients: except the cooking spray and whisk well.

2. Grease a cake pan with the oil, pour the cake mix inside, introduce in the oven and bake at 350ºF for 40 minutes.
3. Cool down, slice and serve.

Garlic chilli prawns with sesame noodles

Ingredients:

- bunch spring onions , thinly sliced lengthways
- 300g bag beansprout
- 4 garlic cloves , finely chopped
- 1 red chilli , finely chopped
- 400g raw peeled tiger prawn
- 1 tbsp soft brown sugar
- 250g medium egg noodle
- 1 tbsp sesame oil , plus extra to serve (optional)
- 1 tbsp groundnut oil
- 1 tbsp dark soy sauce

Directions:

1. Cook the noodles following pack Directions:, then rinse with cold water and drain. Toss with 1 tsp of the sesame oil.
2. Heat 2 tsp of the groundnut oil in a non-stick wok. Stir-fry most of the spring onions and all the beansprouts for a couple of mins until tender.
3. Add the noodles and warm through. Stir through the remaining sesame oil and tip out of the wok onto a serving dish.
4. Carefully wipe out the wok and add the remaining groundnut oil. Toss in the garlic and chilli, and cook for 10 secs.
5. Pop in the prawns and stir-fry for a couple of mins until they have just turned pink. Stir in the sugar and soy, then bubble until the sugar has melted and prawns are cooked through.

6. Spoon on top of the noodles and sprinkle with the remaining spring onions. Add an extra drizzle of sesame oil, if you like.

Superhealthy salmon salad

Ingredients:

- 200g sprouting broccoli , roughly shredded, larger stalks removed
- Juice 1 lemon
- Seeds from 1 a pomegranate
- Small handful pumpkin seeds
- 2 handfuls watercress
- 100g couscous
- 1 tbsp olive oil
- 2 salmon fillets
- Olive oil and extra lemon wedges, to serve

Directions:

1. Heat water in a tier steamer. Season the couscous, then toss with 1 tsp oil. Pour boiling water over the couscous so it covers it by 1cm, then set aside.
2. When the water in the steamer comes to the boil, tip the broccoli into the water, then lay the salmon in the tier above.
3. Cook for 3 mins until the salmon is cooked and the broccoli tender. Drain the broccoli and run it under cold water to cool.
4. Mix together the remaining oil and lemon juice. Toss the broccoli, pomegranate seeds and pumpkin seeds through the couscous with the lemon dressing.
5. At the last moment, roughly chop the watercress and toss through the couscous.
6. Serve with the salmon, lemon wedges for squeezing over and extra olive oil for drizzling, if you like.

Malabar prawns

Ingredients:

- 4 curry leaves
- 2-4 green chillies, halved and deseeded
- 1 onion, finely sliced
- 1 tsp cracked black pepper
- 40g fresh coconut, grated
- 400g raw king prawns
- 2 tsp turmeric
- 3-4 tsp kashmiri chilli powder
- 4 tsp lemon juice, plus a squeeze
- 40g ginger, half peeled and grated, 1 finely sliced into matchsticks

- 1 tbsp vegetable oil

- ½ small bunch coriander , leaves only

Directions:
1. Rinse the prawns in cold water and pat dry. Toss them with the turmeric, chilli powder, lemon juice and grated ginger and set aside.
2. Heat the oil in a pan and add the curry leaves, chilli, sliced ginger and onion.
3. Cook until translucent, about 10 mins, then add the black pepper.
4. Toss the prawns in with any marinade, and stir-fry until cooked, about 2 mins.
5. Season if required and add a squeeze of lemon juice. Serve sprinkled with the coconut and coriander leaves.

Zucchini noodles with vegetables and sour cream

Ingredients:

- Clove of garlic
- 200g cocktail tomatoes
- 2 tbsp sour cream
- 2 tablespoons of olive oil
- 800g zucchini
- 1 yellow pepper
- 2 spring onions
- Olives
- Salt
- Pepper

Directions:

1. Cut the zucchini into pasta with a spiral cutter.
2. Dice the bell pepper and cut the spring onion into rings. Halve the tomatoes and chop the garlic.
3. Heat the oil in a pan and fry the zucchini noodles. Now stir in the remaining vegetables, add sour cream and season to taste.

www.ingramcontent.com/pod-product-compliance
Lightning Source LLC
LaVergne TN
LVHW021239080526
838199LV00088B/4750